Heat Lines

D1202623

Heat Lines

MICHAEL ANANIA

ASPHODEL PRESS | KINGSTON, RHODE ISLAND & LANCASTER, ENGLAND

For purchasers of this book, an audio file or CD-ROM is available
for a nominal sum. Call the number below to order a copy.

Published by Moyer Bell
Copyright © 2000, 2001, 2002, 2003, 2004 by Michael Anania

All rights reserved. No part of this publication may be reproduced or transmit-
ted in any form or by any means electronic or mechanical, including photocopy-
ing, recording or any information retrieval system, without permission in writ-
ing from Moyer Bell, 549 Old North Road, Kingston, Rhode Island 02881
or Moyer Bell c/o Gazelle Book Services Ltd., Falcon House, Queen Square,
Lancaster LA1 1RN England.

Grateful acknowledgement is made to the following publications in which some
of these poems first appeared: *Notre Dame Review, Chicago Review, Samisdat, Erbe
d'Arno, Blue Sky, Near South, Square One, In Print, UIC Alumni Magazine, Powerlines, The
Literary Review The Gathering of the Tribes* and *Café Review.*
"Garden Pieces" first appeared in *Chicago Review.*

Poems in this collection were also published in Haybarn Press limited editions,
Once Again, Flowered, Sounds/Snow, and Poems of Sea and Land with drawings and lith-
ographs by Ed Colker. "Rain Dancing" was first published as a broadside by
The Poetry Center of Chicago.

First Printing, 2006

LIBRARY OF CONGRESS
CATALOGING-IN-PUBLICATION DATA

Anania, Michael, 1919-
Heat Lines

p.   cm.
I. Title   2006
PS3551.N25H43   2006-023220
811'.54—DC22   CIP
ISBN: 1-55921-384-1 (paperbound : alk. paper)

Printed in the United States of America
Distributed in North America by Acorn Alliance,
549 Old North Road, Kingston, Rhode Island 02881,
401-783-5480, www.moyerbellbooks.com and
in the United Kingdom, Eire, and Europe by
Gazelle Book Services Ltd.,
White Cross Mills, High Town,
Lancaster LA1 1RN England,
1-44-1524-68765, www.gazellebooks.co.uk

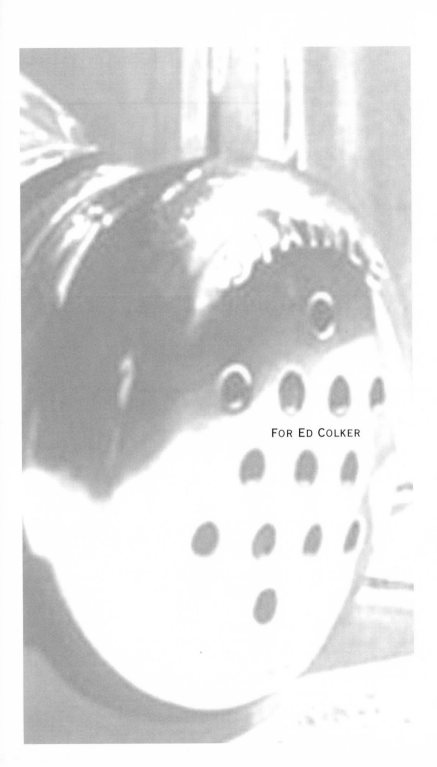

FOR ED COLKER

Contents

"The fundamental question remains, How do we add content to the notion of bare activity?"
—Alfred North Whitehead

" . . . any shape on the delicate air will suffice."
—Ken Smith

I

STEAL AWAY

"the dead are caretakers"
Jeffrey Allen

in the end, at the ending
everything retreats; farewell
daylight and all your objects;

the Jeffrey bus rocks around
the curve below my window
its cabinet of artificial light;

sing the lionheaded storefront
lost to discount gas pumps,
barbershop—Leon!—whispered

away; who died here, shanked
on his way to play the blues,
Sterling? chorus gone silent;

I remember Curtis rounding
his round face with a smile,
Super Fly, can you see him

outlined in the plaster clinging
to an exposed brick wall,
the remnants of one house

illustrating another, stained
wallpaper fresco, its sainthood,
a dream grown arms, legs,

dance step in silhouette;
are they sad, then, sad captains
of sad songs? "can you," he says,

"can you dig it," or will you
(it no longer seems to be
a question); Sonny Boy

and Curtis, each smile
peaked church roof prisms
the distance; south, you say,

on Indiana, toward Teresa's,
pigs' ears on Wonder Bread,
"a slice of life, honey," the lines

in her palms like squid ink
drawn across parchment, sepia,
of course, no more, no less;

who was it, then, the sodium lights
yellowing toward evening; looks
can be deceiving; the stroll, not

so much as raised his hand
or dipped his head to say hello,
calluses zinging across strings,

blind, perhaps, or playing,
someone said, just like a blind
man, or learned to play watching

a blind man play, blind lemon
branching from a blind tree,
Leon, and so seems that way,

all sound without sight,
without sight reading, the exact
dip of head and shoulders,

stroll just past where the El
screeches out his name; can you
(the question is its own answer)

see him, Sonny Boy gone
to shadows, Superfly, can you
reach into the moist coil

the song leaves turning
in the night air, its bright
scales chilling your fingers,

uncoils, then recoils,
tongue flicking the lilt
things sometimes take,

names passing by, arms
shoo-bopping, heel cleats
drag out the beat, coils

in the night's ear, song;
can you see, just there
like a paper cut-out;

Little Walter going this way,
Blind Lemon, that? St.James'
steeple and Olivet's stone face;

Eunice said, look here,
it doesn't matter what you
think or who you think you are;

there's man crouched behind
a bureau with two children
and a loaded gun thinks

you're the way back from
too far and all that matters
is that he thinks you are;

at some point in our lives
we might each of us be called
upon to be what we seem;

Superfly, accidental saint
suspended above churchfronts
and on-coming headlights,

say what it is that's
rung out track after track,
the brightness steel work

leaves across steel, names,
or how too far's edge draws
us along like a third rail,

its sparks opening quick
constellations, their sudden
horoscopes etched into

the backs of our eyes, lines,
names like hands raised in song,
moist sepia drawing in the half-light,

stroll, Oliver, Hines, Armstrong,
One Hundred and One Changes
down the line, names, how

they ring, Superfly, can you
see him, Sonny Boy, Sterling,
the chord dead fingers clutch

at in the summer air, moist
as song and sacrament, Leon,
the figure in paper and plaster,

can you see him in flight
or the body, hand stretching
toward song, folded into a doorway?

listen up, listen up! too far
is a song and dance, is hands
raised, is coil and rail returning

SUMMER NIGHT

(Nebraska, circa 1957)

I.

passing through Elmwood, its
single amber warning light swaying
above the pavement; August; stray

wings and bug smears jewel
the windshield, the 1948
Oldsmobile radio clutching

distant musics, its reach
scraped along the prairie's
flat water shale; suddenly

empty, this summer night,
the vague constellations,
cornrows spinning away;

II.

it's Miles, in retrospect
of course, and Gil Evans,
the thin line the trumpet

draws along the horizon,
one darkness defining
another, and clarity,

the song, *songs*, receding
and intermittent, play
prairie grasses back at us,

Kansas City, Omaha,
distances diminished, cool
in the horn's muted restraint;

III.

going home or nowhere
in particular, the night air
greened with cooked alfalfa,

new world sharp and stinging,
Ponca and Pawnee quick as
thought among the cottonwoods;

belongs, the song argues,
where the music takes you,
each measure measuring

out its own place, syllables,
summer night, or a static
hiss, empty and disquieting;

IV.

somewhere north of Palmyra
heading east, crossing
and recrossing the river's

meander; the highway
lifts and falls, sound, then
silence, the land's shadows

interrupting musics
we play ourselves into,
doing 70, at least;

"speak up, I can't remember
your name," so many years,
hand, arm, bracelet and bare knee;

V.

like a pebble dropped in
still water, pebbles, each note
flashing rings in the dark

in time, that time or this,
Chicago in its own moment,
fingertips, yours, stroking the air

across the radio's chrome grillwork,
the fret-lines of numbered light,
whitewalls strumming warm asphalt;

the blues reckoning evenings
north and east, by starlight
and city dancers slick with sweat;

VI.

summer at rest in the past,
Miles, Evans, Highway 2,
each present always merely

remembered, its particles
rearranged, car radio,
prairie, a knee raised only

slightly, the tick of night
bugs swirled up against glass,
death trailed off or fluttering,

Elmwood, recalled for no
reason, its one traffic light,
a crystal pulsing crystal song

A GEORGIC

for Marvin Bell

Virgil talked of corn, of farmers
at their work, the shadows that move
up their hillsides at evening, rain,
sunlight after rain and cloudless skies,
of plants that rise up unbidden
and bare no fruit, birds and their plunder,
salt land and gravel and rich soil
that falls black from the plow's shear,
of land fat and glad with moisture,
of stubble left fallow and the crust
on unstirred fields, fierce sun and frostbite,
how, in time, the crop levels the furrow,
how mildew devours the corn's stalks
how thistle and burs can overcome a crop,
and of the farmer at home, sweet children
clinging to his knees, the holidays kept
and the sacred piety of his household.
Under the shade of a spreading beech
Virgil sang of fields and flocks and trees,
of bees among ripening apples, shrill
locusts, hay-lofts and brimming water troughs
and thought of tillers marched away, the plow's
measure of honor gone, of Caesar bending
sickles into stiff swordblades and hurling
war's lightnings at the high Euphrates.

OBJECTS IN A ROW:
KEN SMITH, READING

three stones, one blue feather,
a piece of polished driftwood,
thin and white as bone, two

shells, convex and dark at their
centers, like eyes lifted out of
the sea; each thing accounted for,

named, then set down along
the front edge of the table, stone,
driftwood, feather and seashell

horizon; his palms opened out,
everything, that is, shown,
given up to table, sightline, speech;

pages lifted into the long reach
of breath in flight: "birds, trees,
men & women," each small sound

cupped and lifted to the ear's driftwood
plate, "the world declaring itself"
landscape   moment   distance   whole

RAIN DANCING

after Diane Reeves

settle it, then,
   the syllable snapped
      between your finger

and your thumb,
   skidding briefly and
      spun, a wooden top

wobbling across
   an uneven floor,
      sound as certain as

rain dancing,
   spirit after spirit,
      random, predictable

and strange, leaves
   in their own sweet time
      and frequent melody

CERTAIN VARIATIONS

for C.S.Giscombe

i.

Tracked or trekked
 along a river's edge,
  swell, surge, siltlines

shoulder high. Here,
 perhaps, a tracing on
  water, wind's wake

against the bending
 sheen of the brown
  current, wavelets

quick as anything,
 leafshade and sunlight
  changing places as you

go, steps moving
 northward, the afternoon
  intermittent and narrowing.

ii.

Landfall and direction
    are, in the end,
        incompatible; ways

tangled with exposed roots,
    the branch that bends
        across your waist, foot

path runnelled and slipping
    away. Turn and turn again.
        There's no point in counting.

Keep the sun to your
    left, they said, river
        to your right; your

heading is approximate,
    no chance of running
        the river's long axis

through these meanderings.
    Summer lifts moisture
        the water renews in marl,

your face wet with it,
   arms and back streaming,
      each step unsteady, dark mud,

like axle grease, spread
   over the under-bedding,
      impermeable, yellow clay.

iii.

Everywhere is beginning
    again, chalklines on concrete,
        each numbered section, a place

to be. Hop hop, then
    with both feet falling
        together, turn back spinning.

Names and numbers,
    a bit of necklace chain
        or ankle bracelet marks

your progress. Pick it
    up without falling; move
        on, along. The end is in sight,

clothesline rope ticking
    the pavement and curtains
        pulled out of their windows.

iv.

Humming along. She
     hummed as she walked,
          the words to the song

not so much uncertain
     or lost as not yet brought
          to mind; sun streaking

the block of ice that
     bounced against the back
          of her red wagon, pale

fault-lines in the ice
     flared like the northern
          lights, her heels dragging,

water running a thin
     trail up the alley, the trail
          itself gathered in by the sun.

Afternoon, Miz Givens.
     Afternoon, she says, her
          voice bobbing in her song.

River—river washed
    and carried and crossed
        over—sprung from mountains

of light sheeted in
    ice. Belongs to whoever
        proposes words the song

might accept, scuffing
    and singing—*how long,*
        how long—and edgeways,

a cool skids by on bright cleats,
    head dipping, his arms' back beat
        moving along the far side of her music..

v.

Out of the landscape
   or waking into its lift
      and fall, treeline heaving.

vi.

Contrails spread bright
    crystals across the sky,
        so many remnants feathering

one determination
    across another, the late sun
        washing them through with

pale colors, pinks
    darkening, minute by
        minute, toward shadow.

Chinese elms, ailanthus,
    locust trees stir, the four
        o'clocks straining westward.

vii.

Is there a moment
    of beginning or a first
        stage, the journey opening

outward like a vista
    seen briefly in the space
        between one hill and the next

or pushed back across
    your face, a sudden rush
        of air you lift out of stillness

like a bow wave, dense
    with brown soil and foaming?
        Apprehension is seeing and

holding. You clutch the handle
    at the corner of the seat just
        ahead of you, waiting for the lurch

the train makes, couplings
    seizing at couplings, under
        carriage jerking the car, your

spine pressed back into
    the brown seat, fingers straining,
        head rocked back and forth.

On your way, under way,
    everything moving backward,
        all that you are passing is past,

moment by moment.
    Moment is the arc of one
        force exceeding another,

implying movement.
    Moment is your place
        in time, is stillness, then.

viii.

Imagining yourself
    begins your self again,
        assumes a time in time's

long swirls, the turns
    and eddying here briefly
        paused as if beginning,

the train or with a sigh,
    the Greyhound bus starting,
        starting out, a chord played

across your spine. Ready,
    get set, already gone, passing
        the lamp post, the street sign,

someone leaning in shadows,
    a flowered dress—think of it—
        sleeves puffed, hemline waving

blossom after blossom.
　　Goodbye street names
　　　　spinning past and bridges,

neither here nor there,
　　like sound boxes, hollowed
　　　　out and deeply echoing.

ix.

"Drags forward its
    beautifully flowing
        breathings." River

once again, flowered
    perhaps, the woman
        seen in passing, pulling

a block of ice, quick
    with sunlight, so much
        stirring through her, blooms

you might say, the sheer
    geometries of summer gauzed
        in silken heat lines around her.

Is, then, by modification,
    a stream gardening as it
        goes. Proposes change,

certainly, the scene
    mirrored along warped
        surfaces of shimmering ice.

x.

"An effort of intensity,
    thick as air," so that
        moving homeward or away

is an action conscious
    of temporal inertias; you
        strain, as though speaking

a second language, not
    merely for words but for
        a sense of yourself moving,

river polished as much by
    memory as light, the trail you
        take always partially overgrown

II

THREE WINTER SONGS

"a cupful of syllables"
Angela Jackson

I.

silence and its attendant
   particles, lint spun
      along the windowshade's

bright fissure, morning
   light, the kitchen's moist air
      quavering, crazed radiator,

windowsill, pale velvet,
   untended, brittle African
      violet leaves, hands, fingertips,

syllables paced out
   one breath at a time, against
      the table edge *do sway, do dance*

II.

City! If love is a circle
    and morning is its radius,
        can night be its center

or the darkness that
    surrounds it played at
        or among, as though

it were shaped into
    treeforms and gangways,
        spaces your breath recalls

or footsteps strike
    as you go quickly,
        the passing contours

of bark and brickwork,
    yours by right of
        unprovoked remembering?

whose body is this
    anyway, leaning, whose
        spirit lifts your arms now,

your voice soft
        and unexpected? Child's
            play, these unlit presences

pasts traced in sooted
        snow, bits of bright glass
            held beneath darkened ice,

the way home, the way
        back, alley after alley,
            street names rung out;

center, of course, and perimeter
        bent inward with your
            fingers, and what is held there

and said once again,
        a song, nouns reeling to
            their own sweet whisperings

III.

do sway, do dance—
    fingertips, fingernails
      busy with words,

a song does leaf here,
    and what you say now
      says its flowering, is made

of light and water, snow-
    quick and greening, petalled,
      sepalling syllables

say street, say lamppost,
    brickbat, what was scrawled
      red in gray concrete, called out,

arms asway and bare shoulders
    counting the music, summer, all
      that the snow's pale present

covers, layers in and slows
    rises in your throat and flares
      across the window's chill panes

A STEP AT A TIME

after Mariano Brull

A colored flower,
the moon, I guess,
yellow as a daisy

and the sky, sea-blue,
a hand, like a dancer's
passing, fingernails

fire red, hair drifting
above venereal waves,
lips, of course, of all

sorts, like painted gulls
trembling at the horizon.
This is the hour, isn't it,

when departure folds over,
under, around and through
the simple sense of things,

the ordinary hues of scrub
trees and pale sand, sea
grasses quick as speech.

SUCH MUCH

for Yaak and Ingrid Karsunke

Does the desert wind really whisper
or does it grate across the sand?
People who know deserts have twenty
or more words for such sounds,

some whispering, some grating,
some shuffling like reluctant departures,
some quick as a blade drawn from its scabbard,
some endearing as a sigh, some demanding

as fingertip and thumb rubbed together,
some zipped, some hushed, some rattlesnaked
sideways, some bitter as breath pulled through
clenched teeth, some lilting, some swinging

like Dizzy playing palm against palm,
some wrought like a drummer's brush on brass,
some eased like hair across fresh linen,
some billowed, some taut, some feathered

across bright strings, some certain as air,
some humming like the nighttime city,
some secret as thighs crossing nylon over nylon,
some wingéd, some gilled, some lidless and strange,

some quavering among heat lines, some suddenly
chilled, some deliberate as bare feet on stone,
some unexpected as beard stubble on satin,
some stammering as a nib pen, some plain

as tapwater, some red and urgent as
bright fingernails clutching flowered
upholstery, some thick as callused hands
on bare wood, some several as leaves,

some counting out a rest and busily waiting
as a spit valve opened and sputtering,
some final as a round spade in dry soil,
some sibilant, wordless, initial syllable

for the traveler listening in the dark
or the agent scribbling ciphers
in lemon juice on soluble paper.
"Such much?" she asked, the Sahara

furled like drapery behind her.
"Much much," he replied, recalling
the slim margin of damp sand hissing
between the long desert and the persistent sea.

AUGUST INTERIOR

Of course the flowers wilt
  with or without us, irises
    darkening back into themselves,

the gladiolas gone to brittle
  paper, spotted lily petals
    fallen in the summer quiet

of the front hallway, the air's
  warm particles suspended between
    perfumed lily and the lily's decay.

Still, absence, yours or mine, seems
  to move it all along, colors once
    brimmed outward, now easing away.

PAPER WHITES

"against the light"
James Schuyler

forced, we say,
bulbs pressed
into damp pea
gravel, roots
pale and spidering;

blossoms against
winter light
each December,
as though in
ceremony, lift

themselves crown
after crown,
weighted flake-
white *impasto*,
snow sun-struck,

your fingers gone
strange now, nerves
stung and tingling,
each touch, crystal
petalled and electric

CHINATOWN

for Bill Russo

it's how they
said it, like
"Tangerine"
or "Cherokee,"

in Bridgeport,
that is—*Chinatown*;
"where you from?"
meaning, what

neighborhood, what
street-corner;
Chinatown, a
privilege;

more certain than
Taylor Street,
deeper, perhaps,
by misdirection,

not Chinese, in
any sense, not
Chinatown proper,
merely adjacent

to it, but meaning
something else
altogether, a special
sense, not of place

but of value, value
acquired in place,
acquiring place,
as in *Chinatown*

CERTAINLY

for Raymond Federman

Dew tempts, per dew.
Is this the garland
of morning or part
of an autobiography?

Someone, not especially
noteworthy in any other
terms, trips and falls,
ripe melons, apples

reaching toward his
hand, though he had
stretched it there
more or less without

choice, an autonomic
reflex to falling,
something that begins
past speech in the inner

ear as gravity's silent
voice. Or a staircase,
perhaps, his palms
and their discreet

monograms extended.
"This is your lifeline,"
she said once, tracing
her own chill across it.

Treads and risers,
future tense implicit,
the worn carpet's
threadbare flowers

everyone who ever climbed
into your past is passing
along the worn edges of
your fall. The imperative

mode freshly invented
for this occasion.
"Run," someone said
in a voice so familiar

you could have mistaken
it for your own. "Hide."
Words, unbidden, out of
another narrowing dark,

meanwhile goes on
and on like a tune
caught in your head
and reeling there, mean-

while continues consonant
by consonant, whispering,
a part of speech with its own
complexly declined inflections,

What language is this, who
walks this way, talks along
serifed letters, sounds adrift,
tic tic—was that a second,

a minute? years, even?—
tock. "More or less,"
she said. Which she? Anyone?
The palmist scooping out the

life in your hand with her
fingernail or another self
you have hidden in your self,
who speaks, as you would,

across the doorsill into
its wedge of light, shadows
passing like random footsteps,
now and then, in tongues.

III

FOUR POEMS FROM ADAMI, CALABRIA (ITALY)

"ppe' tiempu e luntannanzu"

Michele Pane

CARMELO'S GARDEN

Pears and figs. Plots of
red soil turned by hand
from string beans to potatoes,
all fallow now. October
mountain air, bright sun.

Carmelo reaches fresh figs
down to us, soft and purple
at their stems. We bite into
the flowers they clutch inside,
their juices still stained with them.

Under the pear tree next to
his potting shed, mid-mountain,
he cuts pear stems—fingertips
for figs, opened palms for pears—
arms raised as in dance and praise.

Filomena's Hearth

Fire and focus. She sits
at the side of her hearth,
feet together, hands
unimaginably still, two
cured logs angled in.

We speak into the fire,
all that we say eased
upward as smoke, what
Pane called the "hearth's
tongues" slipped in among

pine fronds and chestnut
branches, mountainside
hazed through with speech,
say light as lately situated,
names liquid quick and rising

shadows insistences. This is
the place, after all, said as we
say it, tongues of fire, Filomena,
tended and tended, hands at rest,
feet set on an ancient stone floor.

FELICE'S ALBUM

Pictures and pieces. Time's
diagrams in face and hands,
what marks our way as breaks
and crevices coursed through red
soil and stone make way for water.

Felice in Des Moines under
the eaves of a mid-American
frame house, in Australia beside
a burro, here or there along
the right-of-way from Cosenza

to Catanzaro, Rock Island
and Burlington to Omaha,
one step after another, rail
end to rail end, gandy-dancing,
cross-ties blackened with pitch.

It is the way he walks us up
this vicolo, shoulders still
weighing the rail, hands curled
to it—the work, *lavoru addamaru*—
a small patch of tilled red soil,

flowers and vegetables at hand.
He holds my arm and speaks
in Calabrese, certain in his touch
that I can understand him. We are
brunacchio, he says, bears together,

bearers, meant to carry and set down,
the railroad tie a threshold only from
one moment to the next. This close
passage, he says, lifting his palms
up to stone houses, is history.

Raffaele's Table

Words and words. Dark, small
grapes we kiss onto our tongues,
pinwheel mushrooms, porcini,
roasted chestnuts rolled in news-
print, shedding their papery husks.

As sweet as, as fresh as, as old as
steep hillside shadows, *umbrae*,
the word for—in Latin, in Calabrese—
those other dinner guests just past
the lamplight at Roman tables,

Augustus' poets and ours waiting
their turn to speak in your voice,
Raffaele, or falter in mine, *legge*,
as you say it, keeping garden
and table, the spaces between

this light and those shadows,
page and print, table and room,
house and shadowed valley,
pina calabra going from green
to black each evening, inked

there or feathered, night passages,
lines speaking the past's inflections,
all that was said here shaded in speech,
as the moving shadows of mountain
ledge or pine tree give time to light.

The dark remnants of chestnut hulls,
like bits of letters, broken fonts
scattered across the day's news,
the poem restless in its place,
chestnut meats in our mouths.

TURNINGS

for Enzo Agostino (1937-
2003)

"e ca trovamu 'a luci d'a' memoria"

I.

Evening is liquid here,
    shadows welling into each shape,
        each valley, cut and crevice,

the sky, still bright, its lapis
    sun-streaked, the sea—both seas—
        darkening past Homer. "So soon

as the spirit has left the light,"
    rectangular slips of gold,
        embossed, their Greek, somewhat

Italic, found at Thurii
    and Piercastello-Laquari,
        suspended now behind glass

in the castello at Vibo Valentia,
    charms hammered, as though of fire
        and light, the sun offered back

to the dark flood, "so soon?
    on the right side of Ennoia,"
        a spring, in thought, that is,

lifting itself up out of
    memory. Though the reading
        is somewhat doubtful, folds

in the gold leaf obliterating
    letters, parts of letters, words,
        the sense is clear, prayer

and safe passage, "pure," it says,
    "from pure to Purity, I come,"
        gold out of earth and fire, speech,

spirit in light returning,
    suppliant in her "blessed
        company," funeral offerings,

of course, but folded and carried
    by Greeks at the Calabrian edge of Greece,
        the half-day journey from sea-froth

to sea-froth, following one river
upstream, the other down,
from Temesa and Hipponium

to Schilletion and Petelia,
merchants and colonists, death
touched each evening, rising

sounds and stirrings, the Sila's
mountains, caves and streams
—*Aquavona, Riventinu*—

rough passages that saddle
deep into shadow, chestnut
burs murmuring over leaf-mold;

in Calabria, *stasira, stanotti,*
Eleusis—"the enfolding
darkness"— is still underfoot.

II.

Or "beautiful, this evening's
    evening," the sea running white
        from Punto Stilo south past Locri,

a sparrow hawk wheeling above
    pebblestone, refuge, pinfeathers
        catch the mountain light, the west still

streaming eastward, out of reach.
    "I am," the gold leaf says, "like you,
        a child of earth and heaven."

Upland, from the tourist littered beach,
    Gioiosa—Gejusa—the sun plays
        its last, small strains, like mandolin

music, starlight and sound enshadowed
    there, your spirit drowsing, cradled
        at its home, in speech and light.

III.

A spindle-full of flax, its light,
   votive, drawn out and spun,
      bent fingers lifting bright strands,

like filaments from the still air,
   again and again, the olive wood
      bobbin bobbing above her feet.

Her song is whispers, names circling
   names, each one said into her hands,
      the thread, like a rosary

without pause or end, "Enzo,"
   and each other Enzo, Angelo,
      Michele, Dominic, Bruno,

Raffaele, so many passing
   from light into darkness and curled
      into the black folds of her skirt.

WELCOMING THE FIRE

for Ralph Cintron

I.

It is the way of smoke
and the way of slender
trees, of footholds,

the way of young
women grinding corn
and young men passing;

it is what was said
that day, how branches
swayed, who it was

stepped out into
the chill air wrapped
close in bright blankets;

it is the dance
and the dancers,
the Place of Snow

on the Very Top;
"take the pipe of
your father," she said,

"and make smoke so
the clouds will hide our
paths from witches;"

"my grandson," the old
Spider Woman said, "do
as I say," and she placed

a small white feather
under his heart so he
would be light on the air;

it is the way of wind
and clouds, of water,
snow and floods,

wilted corn and reed,
sun, sand and eagle,
the ways of morning

and evening, of speaking
in turn, of sumac offerings
and corn mending the stone.

II.

And where have you been,
Mr. Hambone? Slapping
your way along the walk,

a sidewalk, merely, dust
ground into place by
Goodyear and Firestone

tires, vulcanized, sweet
Venus, all aglow and you,
I suppose, and your song

so persistent, "Hambone,
Hambone," scratching
worn heel cleats across

broken concrete, neon
humming its bright
commerce into place,

double-stitched, double-
soled, side-zippered
blue suede shoes,

just like the song says,
all that you want, then,
finger popping, gone;

"it aint quick work."
he said, "being something
all of a sudden like,"

pop pop shoe bop
or slap thud slap;
music, as it moves,

moves you along,
the beat easing through
here and there, crossing

over and within;
the back of your hand,
then palm to thigh,

fingertips to chest, "in
time," you say, beside
yourself once again.

III.

Or spoons, for that
matter, or bones
whittled from orange

crate slats and smoothed,
or inner tubes pulled
tight over coffee cans

or bare feet on familiar
soil, the quick play of
lamplight on damp hair;

which song, then? what
dance beckons us, fire
after fire, palms or feathers

drawing their smokes
across our faces, self
re-emerging from self?

IV.

The tick of spiders
in her voice, urgent
as his fingertips,

sparks in the air,
reed song over blue
ridgelines, the ferrous

insinuations of autumn,
corn and snow, small
white feather; the reed

trembles a moment,
breathes, perhaps,
limber with spit;

song, after all,
is one way, dance
another; stepped out,

light on the air,
"chew this," word
by word, the women

grinding, young men
passing, a Pontiac
Catalina, like water

drawn across your
palms, sky parted
into bright ripples.

FOUR MEMORIAL PIECES

I.

"Brother Fox," he said, nodding,
and "Brother Bear," the two
of them, legs angled out
across the curb, straight

fresh creases in their
Sunday gabardines,
leaning against a green
1949 Chevrolet.

"Mr. Peebles," they replied,
and he walked on to
nowhere in particular,
the broken sidewalk

clicking beneath his heels
its ordinary, stride tattoo,
Sister Given's crabapple
fluttering bright pink

blossoms all around,
worn tires across the brick
street playing washboard
strokes for an old song.

II.   *(for Roger and Rodney)*

Mrs. Wead at her screen door,
the streetcar's heft, bright
Fords and Chevy's easing by;
evening, like slow sap, gleams

its way down Charles Street;
Friday night two-tone shoes
and patent leather pumps
quick as light on swift water

going by and going by,
music from the storefront
record store jaywalking
between the moving cars.

"S'bout time for you boys
to be home," she said,
as hemlines flicked along,
night-blooming and strange.

III.

The tin sign on the empty
grocery store at 21st & Clark
where the holy rollers met
each Wednesday and Saturday

night and shouted hallelujahs
behind whited over windows,
dinged with bb's and 22's,
said, "Drink Green River."

IV.

"A razor cut is so fine
that nothing is torn away,
and the flesh rises into
its thin space and wells

up there like blood itself.
When the wound heals,
the ridge remains, like a welt."
I believed at seven, perhaps

still do, that what my father
told me was what I needed
to know, that scars are a way
of reading the world. I counted

razor scars for more than
a year, glancing quickly,
then turning away
and stopped at twenty-two.

HEROIC FRAGMENT

When Balls and Otis,
    who were cousins,
        fell on Herman,
who was alone,
    Singing Sam,
        the ragman, said,
"leave them boys alone,"
    meaning Herman, who
        was so big he was called
the Grizzly Bear,
    though Herman
        lost, as usual.

BONJOUR BUFFALO,
A ROMANCE (1964)

PROEM

Three birds, sparrows
twist and turn
beneath a banking

Tri-Pacer, against
a slate of gray sky:
bonjour Buffalo,

it is a winter's romance,
full of snow and ice,
street salt and cinders.

He wakes on Crystal Beach,
his eyes filled with snow,
snow drifts sighing winter

in his ears, stands in his
own snow-shadow under
the white lattice-work

of the roller coaster.
I am akin to light,
he says, blinking

into the crystal glare,
and water, a blue
defraction, sudden as sky

enameled on French
heraldic silver, a scene—
destrier, aller au feu, quickly

sets forth in his own
wonder, snow-crowned
and manteled. Says,

sword-bridge, sword's
edge and bright company
aswirl. Says, drift is my

fealty, determined as
branching hexagonal
crystal coarsings cast

here and there, chance
reconciled briefly in
lamplight, circle spun,

one order recalling
chaos, *pax vobiscum.*
The bridge behind him,

the river's dark luster
gulping in snow and light,
ahead, heel skid, pitch-

pipe tire spun out, neon's
frayed red line, electric blue
veins and transformers humming.

IV

GARDEN PIECES

for Jennifer Moyer

I.

this morning orange
false monarchs
alight on purple star
bursts of allium,
onion-scented, swaying

II.

under a thicket
of pink honeysuckle
white and pale lavender
phlox powder its shadows

III.

bits of the day
move between tree
light and tree shade,
luminous things
turning themselves
on and off and on

IV.

mulberry and pin
cherry suckers
everywhere

V.

blue jay on
a pine bough
just now,
pinetips, frosted
pale green with
soft new needles,
sprung to his weight

VI.

imagine finches
at the branch-ends
of your nervous
system, touch sound
quick and certain

VII.

not wild carrot
this far West,
Wild Bill, but
prairie parsnip
with a sting to its
feathery dark leaves

VIII.

cut back against
spider mites to
next-to-nothing
the daisy tree is
in leaf and budding
yellow once again

IX.

melancholy, I
suppose, each
time we lean hard
against blank
paper as blossomed
out lilac and wisteria
fidget into the light

X.

black ants sticky
with peony sap
pace their hard buds
May after May

XI.

columbine, all
sorrows passed,
offers its
crenellated,
dense petals
like bounty to
the flagstone path

XII.

fingers leaved,
eyes feathered,
a tuft of cotton-
wood seed lingers
under a length
of spruce like some-
thing you just thought
of, definite in its
slow drift but really
neither here nor there

V

AND CALLED TO MIND

Songs along the river's sweep,
tree fronds lift and fall, light
and shadow, faun-quick, here
or there, sun flakes across brown

wavelets: is this a memory?
the bright cottonwood branches,
white seed fluff spun out in its own
diafana, lux, luxury, gods' sport,

I suppose, bright things brightening,
or a hypothesis memory accepts
almost too readily, land and water
wished backward into dream.

This is where we walk out these
notions; past, perfect, you turn
there, just where willow-tips
graze the swaying foxtails;

we have not met and it is years
before you lived there; your feet
stir the river grasses exactly
as they would have, my hand

rests on damp chokecherry stems;
diafana, hair or fingers carding

heat lines tangled in the air.
It is not the place we left; even

the chill along your arm, small
tokens of winter palmed into
moist leaves, occurred or did not
occur elsewhere and at another time.

This is the convention, then, age,
all that is convened backward
into what seems almost certain,
so is always lost, because loss

is what compels it, future and past,
leaf vein shadowed across eyelid,
water drawing the soil into itself,
breath chanced among shaded humus;

drifts, perhaps, so many pieces
kept in place for so long loosening,
your fingertips, their sudden Cheyenne
flowering like shrubs. Rest, then wake,

stretch your hands into the denser green
forested in shade around us; this is the
present touched through an ingathering
of possible selves companied with light.

CONSIDERATIONS IN TIME

for David and Catherine

Imagine stars at their
distances, the still
sky surfacing so
many moments,

constellations, each
thing proposed to
the eye's incessant
diagram, spun out here.

Daffodils are waning
in the wind, tulips
as well, brightly
dismembering, dog-

wood, cloud white,
its branches black
as anthracite, leaves
as yet undefined, chill

evening, the clatter
of chance, change
and brief certainty
gardening the sky.

ONCE KNOWN

i.

rests in the space between
treeforms, the sensible landscape,
not quite at hand, drifts along
this slant of October light

ii

"just a moment," voices, the lilt
of remembered music, dancing,
a skirt out at the hem, blouse
cut from a surplus parachute

iii

is it particle or form, the shape
leaning, as though into a cold
wind, its shadow pulled along,
leaf and leafmold stirring

iv.

Margaret Whiting, perhaps,
kitchen chairs out in the yard,
moon impossibly large, sky
resting in someone's raised fingers

v.

"a sudden chill," she said, rubbing
her arms, leaf rustle, a breath
drawn in between words, "I mean,
after all," as though somehow imagined

vi.

the year tilts into separations, one
leaf after another, the you
in the song, the guise of love,
night's knave, alas, goodbye

vii.

heartsick, though the small tart
apple snaps against her teeth
and the oranging moon grows
inexplicably warm on her cheeks

viii.

as deft as twilight, how it smudges
the undersides of things, the day,
its season turning, the radio gone
on to another predictable, sad song

"IMBUED/WITH LIGHT"

Columbine, its five doves
turned downward or eagle's
talons, *aquilegia*, caught hold of
as a bright instance of air;

Jacob's Ladder, blue petals
ascending, ray after ray;
infused, lit, that is, with
pollen, its soft gold drawn

out as a filament is drawn
across a blue point of fire;
speech, Pindar said, the lyre's strings
pulled taut across the sun.

SILTING UP

they return, don't they,
these incidental
accumulations,

as certain as
anything, the plain
even textures time

seems to amount to,
how what is layered
here or there curves

only slightly like
something swept
into place with

the heel of your
hand, the print
your life line

left in mud balls
long ago or how
the water you lifted

out of water to your
face ran, first, through
your closed fingers,

then down your love
line's quick stream
and slipped away

"THEIR FIGURES PLAIN"

Out of diligence
    and ardor, more or less,
        quick as fingers, notes

adrift along a thread
    of sea foam, light play,
        wave fall, shoreline and birds

spiraling arced silhouettes,
    cloud sweep and close at hand,
        the present, that is, coming on.

SPHERES

after Ungaretti

after the night's tangle,
tendrils coursing—as if
you and I, here or there,
each thing itself unselved,

moist breath, its breadth
enclosed, "if I should
die," kneeling like a
child into fresh linens,

dark bent into dark,
your hair, that space
it holds behind your
ear, speech curled in

and eddying there—what
is it we lift into the morning
light, one clarity or two,
the day billowing toward us

NOW AND THEN

Better to have seen it slipping away, dancing like a
    bobber in quick water, I suppose, than merely
    to have imagined its luster as the skin of some
    other occasion;
occasion, how curious, when he had meant arm or
    was it calf, either perhaps, the way they are
    drawn tight as the muscles flex and unflex
    beneath them and the alternating ten sions
    seem like satin in the light, which is to say,
    things are conditioned in multiples   or by mul-
    tiples—light, tension, moisture, the long
    accommodations of texture and hue to sun-
    light, one generation after another
he thought the edges of things mattered, said so at
    various times, the precision with which volume
    subsides to line—the pipe fence, for example,
    against the privet hedge's uneven greenery or the
    water tower's side cut out across the afternoon
    sky, sycamore at sunset, the city's motley of
    rooftops;
line, he said, is always consoling, and line, experien
    tially at least, is edge, so arm against uphol-
    stery is line, hair on water, the thin blade of
    sunlit dust fallen from the window shade in
    summer, horizons of all sorts, shoulder, neck,
    the sea's lift against morning or evening, one
    color giving shape to another;

he was going to say, movement is the key, the way
        one thing passes another and how each
        acquires a fresh clarity in the process; that
        sense of the real we attribute, for convenience
        sake, to individual objects is never quite per-
        suasive;
the thing in itself, jingling its telltale silver bell, is a
        fairy tale certainly, alone in some undifferenti-
        ated space, wishing for recognition, a word, for
        example, or an idea warmly wrapped around it,
        some Gretel, at least, to share its apprehension;
no, it's things, never by themselves, never entirely
        still, the lines between them cleaving shape
        against shape, property against property, so you
        and I, he said, or you and the white sand beach,
        waves incessant, treeline nodding palm fronds
        this way and that, what passes in the slow
        clockwork of shadows, move both separately
        and together, even when I am merely propped
        up on one elbow watching you.

IN EDGES, THEN

i.

in jagged light
   this paradise, flash
      after quick flash,

like headlights through
   bridge abutments, the
      retina's slow recovery

or glass shattering
   its own surface tensions,
      shard succeeding shard;

dream the intervals away!
   a terrain of longing, then,
      landscape in sudden relief;

it is a body, isn't it?
   pelvis like a promontory,
      I suppose, seen sideways

and arms, legs, the folds
   of linens warm with sleep,
      between you and the window

where the traffic chatters
    its epic cinema, stars a-twinkle,
        Paramount and Orpheum, such

diligent remembrance, *sempiterna*;
    the light fails, certainly,
        but the desire remains,

its satin liquid lusters
    streaming and streaming
        along the slopes of skin;

ii.

this is not a movie,
   at least, not necessarily
      so, the city quick and familiar

against whatever offers it
   a convenient translucence,
      windowshade or eyelid, how

desire hankers across
   intermittent darknesses,
      not so much for stories

but for continuities, even
   in momentary time; and Gilda,
      the implicit flow of light along

her nightgown, each breath
   proposing the next as footstep
      proposes footstep or word word,

night's long road
   opening, turn after turn,
      to the headlights' sweep;

it is all projection, here,
      there, what sleep, when it comes,
            presses back at you, your self cupped

in the unintended shape your
      hand takes when it has nothing
            to clutch at or recall, blood surging

its own constellation of busy
      particles across the glazed
            backs of your eyes themselves

NOTES

"Steal Away":

    Set on the Near South Side of Chicago, the storefront building described occupied 31st Street between Michigan and Indiana. The block was a part of the area of bars and jazz clubs in the 1920s called The Stroll and included the Lincoln Gardens, where King Oliver's band with Louis Armstrong played. The poem's music history comes from William Howland Kenny, *Chicago Jazz: A Cultural History, 1904-1930* and Charles Keil, *Urban Blues* and from conversations with Leon Forrest and Sterling Plump.

Curtis, composer, arranger, singer Curtis Mayfield (1942-1999)

Superfly, main character in the 1972 film for which Mayfield wrote the title song and the score

Sonny Boy, John Lee "Sonny Boy" Williamson (1914-1948), blues harmonica player, murdered on his way to (or from) the Plantation Club in 1948

Teresa's, blues bar on South Indiana in the 1970s and 80s

Marion Walter "Little Walter" Jacobs (1930-1968) and Blind Lemon Jefferson (1897-1929) also died in the Chicago streets, Little Walter in a street fight in 1968 and Jefferson under mysterious circumstances in 1929

Hines, Earl "Fatha" Hines was another of The Stroll's musicians

"One Hundred and One Changes" ?for *Jazz Cornet*, Louis Armstrong's first book.

"A Step at a Time": after Mariano Brull's "Canto Rodondo."

"Four Poems from Adami":
Adami is the mountain village in Calabria (P. di Catanzaro) of my father's family. Carmelo, Philomena, Felice and Raffaele are all members of my extended, Calabrian family.

Michele Pane, Calbrian poet (1876-1953), also from Adami, wrote in the Calabrian dialect.

"ppe' tiempu e luntananzu" ("through time and distance"), from Pane's *"A mia figlia Libertá"*

"lavoru adamaru," adamaru is Pane's term for natives of Adami, so their work and their manner of construction, as in *lavoro Romanum.*

"*brunacchio,*" literally, bronzed or burnished; in
Felice's sense, bear-like, workers.

"*umbrae,*" as a term for the peripheral guests at
Imperial dinners, from Suetonius, though the
word survives into modern Calabrese.

"*pina calabra,*" the pine tree of the Calabrian forests.

"Turnings":
Enzo Agostino, Italian (from Gioiosa Jonica,
Calabria) poet and teacher, who wrote in
Calabrese and Italian.

"*e ca trovamu?. . . ,*" "and that I will find [there] the
light of memory," from Agostino's "Primavera"
in *Coccia nt"o' Gramoni* (2003).

"Homer," both Calabrian coasts, Tyrrhenian and
Ionian, appear in the *Odyssey*.

"So soon as the spirit?," from the gold leaf Orphic
Lamella in the museum at Vibo Valentia (the
ancient Greek city of Hipponium). The prayer
describes the Underworld, with a cypress tree,
the lake of memory and the fountain of
thought (Ennoia) and invokes Persephone.
These have been found throughout southern
Italy. See Harrison, *Prolegomena to the Study of
Greek Religion*.

Notes

Temesa. . .Petellia, sities in Magna Graecia.

Aristotle described the northern border of Magna
   Graecia as a half-day journey along the Amato
   and Corace rivers from Lemetia on the Gulf of
   St. Eufemia to Schilletion on the Gulf of
   Squillace.

Aquavona, Riventinu, sites in the Calabrian moun-
   tains.

"*stasira, stanotti,*" from Agostino's Calabrese, "this
   evening, tonight."

"the enfolding darkness," from the lamella inscrip-
   tions.

"beautiful, this evening's evening," Agostino, "*É bella
   stanotti 'a notatta.*"

"Welcoming the Fire":
   Title and the lore in Part I, from Frank Waters,
   The Book of the Hopi and Mary Elting, *The Hopi
   Way.*

Hambone, both the name of the rhythmic hand
   and a body music described and the central
   character in the accompanying songs
   ("Hambone, Hambone, where you been?").

"spoons?bones?coffee cans," home-made percussion instruments.

"And Called to Mind":
  "lux in diafana," (light in transparency), see Canto XCIII

"Once Known":
  "a surplus parachute," during WWII and after parachute silk was used to make women's clothing

"Margaret Whiting. 1940s popular big band singer

"Imbued/with light":
  title from Charles Olson, Maximus III

aquilegia (from "eagle") is the botanical name for columbine (from "dove")

"Spheres":
  after Giuseppe Ungaretti's "Preghiera" from *Prime* (1919)

"In Edges, Then":
  "Gilda," the title character, played by Rita Hayworth, in the 1946 King Vidor film.

COLOPHON

Michael Anania is a writer, editor and was a professor at the University of Illinois, Chicago. He has won a number of awards for his writing including the Friends of Literature Poetry Prize, a Best American Short Stories Award, a Pushcart Prize in Poetry and Criticism and art council literary awards and fellowships in poetry, fiction and criticism. The lives in Chicago and Austin.

The text of this book was set in Centaur, a typeface designed by Bruce Rogers (1870-1957). Consid-ered one of America best designers, Rogers was influenced by the work of William Morris and the Arts and Crafts movement. His magnum opus was the *Oxford Lectern Bible* set in Centaur. The poem titles are set in Trajan and the folios are Sabon SC. The display faces in the front matter are Broadway Engraved BT and Copperplate 29bc.

Heat Lines was typeset by Rhode Island Book Composition, Kingston, Rhode Island and printed by Versa Press, East Peoria, Illinois. The cover and text paper is acid-free.